Colored
Boy

POEMS AND
ONE ACT PLAYS
GROWING UP
"COLORED"

Colored
Boy LIFE THROUGH
COLORED EYES

Carlo Orto

This publication is in the category of: African-American Poetry and Plays, Minority Poetry and Plays, War Poetry, Civil Rights Poetry and Plays, Hispanic-Puerto Rican-Borinquen-Latinx Poetry and Plays, History of Minorities in America through Poetry and Plays, Modern Poetry and Plays, and American Poetry and Plays.

This is a product of THE KING'S GARDEN literary enterprises.
We can be reached by email at N2YQ@arrl.net.

✳

We produce children's books, prose, poetry, fiction, non-fiction, plays, self-help, science, mathematics, and history.

Illustrations by Loretta Scaleata

ISBN 13: 979-8-9999986-9-9

Dedication

These ramblings are dedicated to all the small, big, noisy, dirty, crowded cities and towns around the world, and the souls living in them. These are the places where I have spent time learning about life, humanity, the universe, and ultimately myself. In these cities and towns, at their cafes, bars, jazz clubs, parks, on their buses, trains, and in their libraries, I have written most of this work. These cities and the souls I have encountered there taught me about hate, indifference, and love. Each place and every person contained the secret that no matter where I am, no matter who is with me or not with me, I can still choose love over hate, life over death, and hope over despair.

Particular thanks to Chakmakli-Turkey, Uijeong-bu-South Korea, Mosul-Iraq, and Jerusalem-Israel. I must give special mention to Scalea-Italy that brought my family back to life after COVID and Brooklyn-New York where I took my first breaths and where my beginnings were nurtured by its people, schools, jazz clubs, and streets. Lastly, none of this would have been possible without the love of my wife, Merle, and the children we raised together in this difficult but extraordinary world.

Most of the time a week is just a week, but, sometimes a week is the creation of the world.

Contents

Acknowledgments

All acknowledgments are, at best, incomplete. Many of the people, places, and things that mold and shape us are unknown and often invisible. Despite that, there are people, places, and things that stand out.

In my personal life I was lucky to be born with a caring mother and father and surrounded by siblings that gave me the intelligence and tools to fight through the challenges we all face. Besides my parents and siblings, I was blessed with two wives, Zena who passed away and my present love Merle. They loved and nurtured my wild dreams and visions of what should be but wasn't, but yet could be. Our children, all thirteen, and our grandchildren, all twenty-six, have been the wind below my sails that have sustained and thrust me forward.

Besides my family, there are those outside of it who influenced this work. Many of their names will be mentioned in this work. To all of them, living and dead, I say thank you. Without their courage and sacrifice I, we, would not have been able to see the promised land.

Closer to home, I will never forget Irene and Tony Fernandez who lived on my block on Bergen Street. We spent countless hours around their kitchen table talking race, politics, religion and where I would spend every Christmas eve helping them to wrap their children's presents.

I cannot forget Dr. Owen Mattingly my college astronomy and mathematics professor and his wife Miya. Living in Japan during WWII, she was my first teacher about the horrors of war as she survived the fire bombing of her city. Dr. Mattingly taught me mathematics and together they both taught me how to be kind to myself, and that it was an honor to be a "colored" boy from Brooklyn.

Then there is Bernie Berstein (the gray ghost) our local TV repairman (when we use to fix TVs and radios) who had his repair shop on Atlantic Avenue and Smith Street. There I spent countless hours at night learning electronics, talking about the big world and listening on his shortwave radio to the Morse Code of ships coming and going from the New York Harbor.

It is impossible to put into words the effect that being a Soldier has had on my life and the life of my family. To all the Soldiers I served with, to all that never made it home, to the men and women of the 101st Airborne Division, 502nd STRIKE (Air Assault-Band of Brothers and Sisters) who I had the honor of twice going to war with, to the Cadets of the United States Military Academy at West Point that I had the honor to teach and lead for nine years, I say thank you. You have honored me by letting me stand in your shadow.

A special thanks to Dave Johnson, my poetry teacher at The New School in New York. He made me unafraid to write about the colors of war. He opened my eyes, heart, mind, and ears by showing me the MUSIC OF POETRY.

Lastly to the Cheyenne River Sioux Tribe of the Lakota Nation at Eagle Butte, South Dakota, I say PHILÁMAYAYAPI, thank you. They honored me by allowing me to participate in the funeral of two fallen Lakota Sioux American Soldiers. It was during my visit that the tribe leader made me an honorary Medicine Man. To all of you I say SEE YOU ON THE HIGH GROUND!!

HOOOOOOOOOAAAAH!!

Introduction

OVERVIEW

One may ask, what warrants another book on poetry (that includes one act plays). One would think with all of our problems of diseases, wars, famines, earthquakes, assassinations, worldwide hate and discrimination that perhaps a book that offered solutions on one of these topics would be more appropriate.

Perhaps that is the point. For those who have not studied history or just lived a few years on this planet, these problems may seem new to a generation just off the press. The unfortunate truth is that these problems are part of humanity's DNA. They are repetitive. Understanding this can help us get a better handle on dealing with them

These poems and one act plays hope to show that the terrain we are walking today is very similar to the terrain we have walked before   As I write this Charlie Kirk has been assassinated, President Trump has had multiple attempted assassinations, political leaders have been shot at and their homes invaded, their families attacked, we have American Soldiers on our city streets, and we are experiencing violent demonstrations and riots.

Though most of these poems talk about past events, the reader cannot help but see similarity with present ones. Under the eye of time and experience, past, present and future often get comingled and become inseparable.

Before I turned eighteen I lived through the beating and killing of Emet Till and Rosa Park's decision not to give up her seat on the bus on that fated cold day in December 1955. I felt the national trauma caused by the assassinations of President Kennedy, Malcom X, Dr. Martin Luther King, Jr., and Senator Robert F. Kennedy. I felt the fear and terror caused by the race riots in Chicago, Los Angeles, Harlem, Detroit, Newark, Washington, D.C.,and church bombing in Birmingham.

I saw on our little black and white television violent demonstrations on college campuses, American Soldiers on our city streets and universities. In Ohio, National Guard Soldiers used live fire on American college students killing four and wounding nine. This list of killings and riots are hardly inclusive of the times.

Many of these poems list places and names of people unfamiliar to most. It is hoped that this will spark an interest in the reader to become more knowledgeable with our common history, remember our wins, and discover new heroes. With this, perhaps not feel despair by knowing that we, as a people, as a Nation have live through and survived such events and have become stronger and more united because of them.

The present is not the past and present events are *not* exact copies of past ones. We have come a long way as a Nation, as a people, and it is unfair to say we have not advanced, have not improved, have not worked the dream. However, it is fair to say that in the present, we have hit more than a few speed bumps in the road. We can learn from the past and hopefully this work will teach us what past generation felt, learned, and did to get out of the cycle of hate, violence, and dysfunctional governance, if only partially, if only temporarily.

SPECIFICS

A note on reading these poems is in order. The reader will notice at least two significant typographical patterns about the forthcoming poetry. The first is the short lines and the second is the unusual spacings.

Some lines will have just one word and some two, three, etc. The lines are short to help the reader focus on the single words and phrases. Words are separated on their own lines to encourage the reader to stop and ask, "What makes this word so special? How does it connect to the previous thought? How does that connect to the following thought?" How does it connect

to other single words in the poem? Some lines may
appear to stop the thought progression altogether. It
is hoped the reader will assume that there is a purpose
here and will be challenged to find it.

This work is lyrical. The reader is encouraged to play
with the phrasing of the words and lines. By doing so,
a variance of meanings will appear. The reader should
stop and savor the words, the phrases as they would
savor a note, the musical phrasing of a piece of jazz.

The reader should should play with the tone, the
word, and enjoy the variations. They should listen to
the phrasing of the words and rephrase them them like
a jazz musician to make their own improv. As Miles
Davis said, "Don't play what's there, play what's not
there." We challenge the reader to do same. Don't just
read what's there, read what's not there. Change the
words, add their own, rearrange the lines, find new
meanings, turn the poem into their own improvisation,
make a tune and sing the words. Make it their own to
discover new rhythms, new truths, a new song.

The second thing to note will be the spacing of lines
of the poems. This is also done to emphasize words,
phrases, and to extend thought beyond the written
script. In either case, I will leave it for the wise reader
to play with the poems and determine if all of this was
worth the effort.

The last point I would like to make is that though many of the events described in these poems are over a half century old and that the emotions and experiences are described through "colored eyes", it does not mean that they are not universal. The reader, regardless of their background, will readily identify with many of these poems not because of color but because of our common humanity.

I, like all writers, would like the world to read these poems and plays. Though poets want to be read, they write for the same reason jazz musicians play. We do this because our soul requires it. We make music and write to understand our soul and the soul of others. We make music and write for the Universe to hear. We make music and write for our souls to heal. We do this even if there are no readers or listeners. We do this because we must.

There are forgotten histories and forgotten heroes in this work. We hope the reader is encouraged to explore this forgotten history and discover some new personal heroes. We hope the reader experiences the thoughts and feelings growing up with "colored eyes," the eyes of a "COLORED BOY". These poems and short plays contain the emotions of fear and courage, hate and love, confusion and vision, as all were present during those times. They are equally present in these times.

Ultimately, it is courage, love, and vision that win out. We challenge the reader to leave behind the fear, the hate, and the confusion but pull out the courage, the vision, the love to see possible solutions for our present challenges and know that is the best way forward.

KEEP THE FAITH, BABY

CHAPTER ONE

Colored Folk

The First Day

langston

was dat deferred
dat waz dreamt
or was ya' colored
by yars father pointin'
outin'
niggers in de field
as ya' rodes dat train
t'rough kansas
dat undiscovered boy

ya' wrotes of colored's
not yet blacks
just negros
african never really americans comes
right bout the time
ya' checks
out

ya' founds slaved freedom
comin' to harlem
d'ough baldwin
gay'd the scare
offs yu' soul
hopin' for de liason

ya' was of afraid

he cames
but
after ya' did
d'ose many times in
alliz hall'wayz
rooftops
anywhere'z away'z
from de cops
baton

was dat ya'
mulatto
bastard of w'ite
but not quite
showing off yu' mongrel self
suicide'd
before yu' lynching

dids ya' blame
yuz mama no good
w'en she ain't had
money not enuf to buy
d'ose milk and eggs for yu'
soul gone home

did ya' learns to swim past
colored
as ya' tries to
nigger
crack dat rock
as ya' finds de w'ites only
simply heaven
in dem harlem clubs

did ya' let yu' candle burns
out
before ya' got
yu' soul gayed ri'te
as ya' played d'ose
tamborines of glory

we'ze still got some dreams
deffered
some dreams full'illed
and maybes yet
we'ze
can get all saved
on de ba'k of some
good ol' killin's and kings
all marked w'it an'
x

ferguson revisited

the rev George lee
shot gunned to the head
fighting for the vote

ol'lamar smith
killed dead by the law
at ten in the morn'
on the courtroom stairs
for orginizin' some
black

emmett louis till
with just fourteen years
.45 to the head
behind a pickup dragged
in a river dumped
for at a gal whistling
white

john earl reese
just turned sixteen
shot while dancing
just for fun reason

with his favorite gal
black

willie edwards junior
with his best friend
mack charlie parker
pushed off a bridge
for maybe dating a
white

ol' herbert lee
father of nine
single shot to the head
blown away by the badge
being rich enough
for dare wanting to vote
black

corporal roman ducksworth
just twenty seven
travelling on a bus
visiting sick wife and child
shot in the chest
a freedom rider maybe
not but surely just
black

young sailor samuel younge
only twenty one
shot in the face
at standard oil fill up
trying to piss in a john for only
white

colonel lemuel penn
world war hero too
driving on home
benning to dc
body shotgunned
not just uppity
but surely a johnson
black

thank you for your service
from a grateful nation
not
all military men
all shot dead
black

brother medgar evers
snipped by le beckwith
in front of wife and kids

for organizin' integration
white living with
black

little
addie may collins
denise mcnair
cynthia wesley
carole robertson
all under fourteen
all coltrane remembered
all abama
all bombed in birmingham
early one sunday morn'
for just going to church
black

james earl chaney
andrew goodman
michael henry schwerner
kkk'ed to the same 'ol grave
the nigger and the kikes
for only believing
black can live with
white

dear viola liuzzo
white
catholic mother of five
down from chitown
shot twice in the head
for driving
back to their homes
some poor boys
black

then they took the best
the doctor
the king martin luther
j   r
right after he said play
take my hand precious
lord
play it really pretty and
sweet
with a thirty aut' six
straight to the cheek
breaking the jaw
cutting the jugular
his face and neck
black

many years later
just one moment ahead
poor michael brown
lay shot on the ground
don't shoot up hands
black

while brother george floyd
saying i can't breath
was taken away
to continue the play
black living together with
white

we play it agin'
agin' an' agin'
like 'dem good old days
making us great

agin' an' agin'

play it again sam

that nigger
skin
dark deep
black
jim crow'd
nine millimeter'd
negro'd down
these main mean
streets

american

back breaking
choke holds
bleeding brown bodies
water hose'd sprayed
roaches poisoned
rats
auschwitz'd jews

left to die

rumain brisbon
thirty four

father of four
threatening with
bottle of pills

not a man

turned just twelve
tamir rice
armed to kill
non automatic gun
bb

boy

michael brown
big eighteen
carrying concealed twinkies
loaded
with the intent to
eat

just a punk

eric garner
forty three father of six
penalty of death

selling dem' loosies
just some cig's
to earn the cash
to just feed his six
kids

no matter just black

pissed on lives
shitted no nothing beings
defecated kids from
brown mother's
wombs

don't they matter

another brother another

murder

    floyd flooding
    our pandemic
    days
    credulous injustice
    taking our breath

away

    leaking life
    from kneed bodies
    on the streets
    of twin cities

burn baby
burn

    sirened cruisers
    once
    cross sheeted

white

    a few blue
    currently costumed
    committing casual
    slow motion

execution

eric'ing black mothered
souls
with exterminational composure
just stepping on
black and brown
roaches

burn
baby burn

covid ghettoed
beings trying
power washing
off their unwanted
color

video'ed over
over
and over
posted on toktiked
or bookfaced
as everyone watches
no one sees
no who
giving a shit

burning babies
burning

jimmy ray

on a grin   i squeezed

shot that blacky
lying in blood
now a good nigre
i ran   laughed
                        country
in
o
        r   t
                i

minutes of
                        mourning
our
        dis   *grace*
i saw   *unseen*

niggar lied in state
other niggars mourning
crying white traitors
on a two muled caisson
the niggar rolls
to his grave in glory

jfkmlkrfk

fuck them   *all*

fuck all niggrurs
all niggrur lovers
the three k's are dead
long live the   *kkk*

we   stand
with a dream deferred
as the king referred

but

the dreamer said
from the mountain top

                        he saw

the promised land
afar

did we miss the
turn
while cleaning

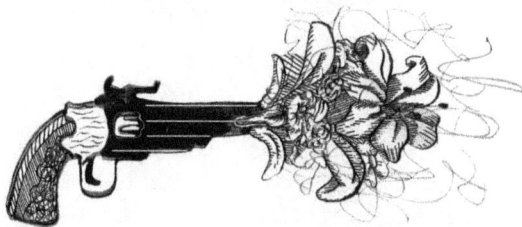

                        our guns

MLK

four four sixty eight
eighteen o'one
forever lost

   laying here
   but not
   here
   i am but
   here
   but to finish
   complete
   the work

feeling
   all
   love given
   warming light surrounds
me
   a blanket
   a shawl
   carrying me on
   home

all journeys
short

end's ending
    not yet
    but all
    all start
    over and over

        i travel
        i leave
        yet i am with you
        always
        always do
        what must be done
        to
        keep on keepin' on
        to get to the promised
        land

        been
        to the mountain top
        been
        to the valley
        of the shadow of
        death

only the
love
can dispel the
hate
can win the

life
now   on my way
                   on my way
                   to the canaan land

                   the chariot swings
low
                   swing the chariot
low
                   carrying me home
                   carrying me on

                          home

mirame dio

mirame dio
mira mi alma
dezolada
por la partida de mi kerida
i yo plantado en esta tierra

mirame sielo
mira mi korason
retirado
komo un pasharo solitario
kon su kante kevrado
sovre el tejado

mirame suelo
mira mis lagrimas
kayendo
sovre tus manos aviertas
onde se avriran las flores mas dulses
de la manyana

mirame dio....

NOTE: *The above poem is written in Ladino (Djudeo-espanyol). It is the language of 1492 Spain, the language the Jews took with them at the Expulsion in 1492. The grammar and spelling reflects its antiquity. It is still spoken in Israel, Turkey, Morocco, etc. It has a long literary (poetry) tradition. Translation by the author follows...*

look at me god

look at me god
look at my soul
desolate
by the parting of my lover
and i1 planted on this earth

look at me heavens
look at my heart
isolated withdrawn
as a solitary bird
with his song broken
on the roof

look at me earth
look at my tears
falling
on your open hands
where the most sweetest flowers
of the morning will open

look at me god....

CHAPTER TWO

Colored Places

The Second Day

ferguson

black
big bear but
boy
not the big
not the bear
it was
the boy
the black
that got killed

me

can't you see
me
can't you see
me a son
can't you see me
a brother
just the fuck see

me

that invisible threat
you
fear the image
you yourself

you
　　　　created in your
　　　　　　head
　　　　　　that is laid on
　　　　　　my soul

　　　　　　solving your problems
　　　　　　of the bogie man
　　　　　　of the black
　　　　　　of the brown
　　　　　　of the colored
　　　　　　of the white

you

　　　　　　the sins of
custer
　　　　　　the indiscretions of
masters
　　　　　　the lash to striking
workers
　　　　　　the maggot'ed indian
meat
　　　　　　the poor white
trash
　　　　　　the dc macarthur'ed mudered
veterans
　　　　　　the bar hall

floosy

    are all tied into
    your image
    of something

i am

    not
    but you need

me

    to be

    assuaging your red

heart

    as colored as my

skin

    as pure as my

love

    for who you

are

    for what you

do

    for what we can

be

    for what we can

build

    for how our children can

live

just the fuck see
just the fuck see

just the fuck see
me

city's lost spring

emptied
streeted souls
moving
in shadowed hostels
darkened by isolation
sickened filled refrigerated
outdoor
morgue containers
discarded shells of disposable
uncolored humanity
mostly unwanted
unintubated
covid colored
souls

staying from each other
finding
salvation's show
behind
multi colored masked
omicroned reflections
of each other
the other

trying to survive
together
in unchorded
harmony

dc metroliner

watching

rain tired
coming
down on the backs
of sombered colored

pigeons

standing on weathered
power lines watching
faces in the acela passing
expressing

riders

worn out
after a day of
seeking
paradoxical truths
suits and stockings
riding expressing
to meritless meetings
buried in mounds of
blackened
deep snowed in memos
hardened
serendipitously hidden in
bifurcated patterns of iced

confusion

raining
tired on columbidaed backed
                              travelers
seated standing strung
in sagging swinging
cars staring
grayed hopes hiding
unacknowledged perverted
morals
intentions bifurcated
oxymoronic desires
of power lies greed

                              watching

pigeons watch
feeted on outside cables
fatigued
not understanding
these
steeled lined parallel paths
these
pecking back travelers
riding
below their skies
leaded
lost

kuwait

sand
brown hard packed
cured over by
thousand thousands boots
humvees prime movers
quickly pressing deeply
into the night
memories
of who were
we

for me a
desert
they say to in
kill

small rounded rocks
white
hot in winter heat sun
worn
softened by rivers
that stopped
flowing
millenium'ed years before
sandaled boots

crushing them
into crystalline earth
sandy silicates
pushed by deep western
winds
quickly erasing my
footprints
as if i was a
memory
in the distant
past

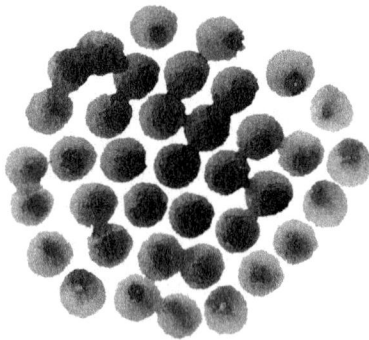

vintage forty second

vialed crack viles
black seamed hookers
high stilettos
pimped
by hatted colored orange
hoods
servicing small
dicked white
boys

fifteen a quickie
five for the mattress
a mirrored room
renting
the quarter hour
if it can stay
hard
between the roaches and bugs
bed

lucy on the street
cool long island lemonade
tripping
molly not even a glint
yet
disemboweling

the flee circus
the late night shows
three big xxx's
for a dollar or nine & nine
or
for two bits four
looped repeated
adult hits sleazed

triple d'ed bra'd
erotic sex hot and
wet
moving on the silver screen
movies
wet dripping succulent
hard'ons
allowing masturbation
in theatres neglected
darkened
way before
the shots of cummings
coming
on cushioned seats
on sticky soda'd floors
trashed

two dogs and a drink
twenty nine cent'

only fifteen empties
at papaya express

down from follies burlesque
tempest and bunny stormed
swinging their nipples
waiting the timing
the gag
blackout

free
to get mugged
hustled hit
cunt conned
or straight street
robbed

then came
the gulianied porn busters
bringing woke laws
along with in laws
to the new crossroads

moving the hood
working the women
the hookers
drugs jacks and jerk offs
to invisible side streets

out of sight
of the euros
where the kids
skelly and hopscotch

now
fucking disney
mickey and minnie
pimping
running their game
taking the green
shooting
pictures with cowboys
naked
feeling you over

almost
gone walking placards
black against white
white against black
on poles up their
ass
writing jesus saves
at the bowery savings

saying repent
see the light
not the neon

if not
then fuck you
die in the fire
freeze in the
ice

butt
stay and get laid
by the uptown
whores
catching a high
tripping
feeling good feeling
bad

great american
honest ol' days

SCALEOTA

nel tuo silenzio
nell'estate della mia anima
ti ho travato
vivendo

vedo i tuoi bambini
giocando
i tuoi genitori
parlando
i tuoi vecchi
sedendo
nei bar e nei caffè
samanta daniela julia alex
i tuoi giovani
chiachierando

in tutte queste cose
trovo il tuo
cuore
sotto le stelle sulle tue
spiagge
sotto le tende sulle tue
terrazze
con il loro bucato
appendo

nei sorrisi
saluti mattutini
via lauro fiume lao
togliatti mancini
e strada marina
le tutte
io camino di sera
notte mattina
impaziente sono di conoscerti
nel rumore del tuo
silenzio
nel silenzio della tua
musica
nella musica del tuo
amore

NOTE: Translation by the author follows.

my scalea

in your silence
in the summer of my soul
i have found you
living

i see your young children
playing
you parents
talking
and your old
sitting
in the bar and in the café
samanta daniela julia alex
and your young
gossiping

in all these things
i find your
heart
under the stars of you
beaches
under the sunshades of your
terraces
with their hanging
wash

in your smiles
morning greetings
on via lauro
fiumo lao
togliatti and mancini
and strada marina
all i walk at evening
night til' morning

impatient to know you
in the noise of your
silence
in the silence of your
music
in the music of your
love

SCALEA

CHAPTER THREE

Colored Times

The Third Day

'92

i
was *discovered*
not being
prior pre-columbian
my non-existent
literature
and satan inspired
numbers
predicted yet to come
events
in the heavens your
superstitions
could only let you blindy
worship

my
books bonfire burnt
unread
by your bible' d numbed
minds
contained answers
to unasked questions
now
forever lost
to my non-existent future

generations

your
bifurcated minds
were unable to understand
not
admit who their own gods were
gods
of silver gold
greed

i
under nature's
duress
offered my own people's
their beating heated hearts
reluctantly
to gods you disapproved
to bring the rains
to feed our men women
children

you
yet you dare condemn me a
pagan
you who offered
willingly
the hearts of

outsiders strangers
jews
men women and children
a-la-stake
whose only crime was
their god was not
a-la-cross

23 de septiembre '68

it
was small
just a puertorican borinquen
revolution
by invitation only
rsvp
in the mountains of the west

jibaros
walking out of lares
out of the jungle
carving
paths to libertad
men
like bent sugar grass
tall
chosen warrior hero'ed
souls
laughing at spanish'ed
masters

awaking to the
dream
singing in tune to the cannon
roaring

marching on that september
before dawn morning
before the earlier cries
grito de ipiranga
grito de dolores
grito de capotillo
grito de yara
brazilian mexican
dominican cuban
now the time of the
borinquen
el grito de lares

brave six hundred
against the empire
at two in the morning
laying their flag
the cross and the star
across the high altar
at the church of lares

the call was sounded
the time to fight
with sharpened machetes
armed with
straw
hat covered heads
path paving pavas

knowing only victory
hoping
but seeing death
following
with bullets against machetes
a proper te deum
before the requiem
crucifixion
of mariana's bandera
the cross and the star

sons and fathers
dead
blood silently crying
loudly
failed freedom familiarity
achieving
the futile attempt to
stand straightened
the nothing
to lose they
lay

jibaros
bodies rotting
on the road from
lares

giving back to the land
red for red

waiting for new young
feet
marching from lares
with pava covered
hearts
walking past fedoras
of suited generations
unidos
singing the song
of lola rodriquez
el grito de lares
se ha de repetir
la libertad awaits us
anxiously
la libertad la libertad

raising again
the cross and the star

'65

mongrel
mixed breed
clean white
filthened by black
birthin'
subversive litters
of no nothin'
people

today tomorrow
forever
segregation on the door
steps standing
protecting rights white
smashed killed indian
babies
in the taking of this land
kkk'ing all other colors
before giving
giving back to
niggers

jimmy lee jackson
shot dead protecting his
mama

not even three fifths
not a man
not allowed to
vote
not permitted to
be

bringing us to bloody
sunday

niggur lover
the white rev reeb
head
billy club mush
payment to all
racial traitors
like ol miss viola
nothing but a bitch
white
catholic mother of five
living the red lettered
bible'd words
shot dead in the head
while driving a cackling
colored boy
and a kettle of kikes
roun' to and fro

ol sheriff clark
calling
the good ol'boys
white
out of dallas county
come get yar
guns
we's huntin' some
coon
open season now
soon
for those niggers
wantin' to be or
just
the vote

just wanna be

now
all of us can
and some of us
don't

16 3 '68

nixoned
by our belief
patrolling
under triple
canopied cannabis
righting high
in the lost
direction

jungled
in our truth
marginalizing
our non-existent gps
while finding gooks
in all the wrong places

they told us
none
existed except we
find
women and children

we mai lai'ed
death
late that late

marching morning
becoming pissed in
calleyed coke cans
our guttered
lives
that rained confetti'd
lies

we lived
and died on busted
gutted
cooperate american futures
being sold to us as
patriotism

onto the next generations
offerings

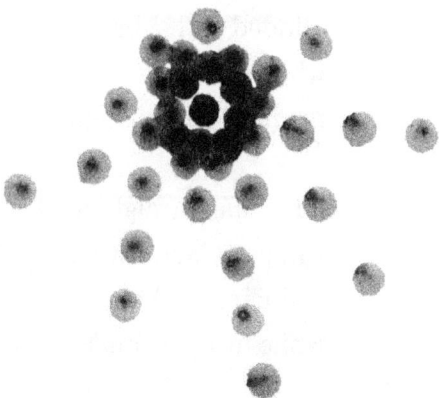

a night's work

roses are fucked
dancing with death
mary's little lamb
met a no good end

blue as his nuts
raining crackers and reds
lynched up for dead
just for a dime

off like a puppet
with lucy in the sky
smoking some shit
while walking a fog

blackboarded jungle
blinded with a bat
while waiting for
the hard white knight

kinky hair straightened
while cooking with iron
white'ing his hide
while firing on ain't

stupid as shit
counting some chickens
without two sense
before they hatch

a stich in the ass
while living in a box
with his head in the ripple
catching the night train express

dumb as a nigger
dirty as a spic
greedy as a kike
drunk like a mick

moving to the back
first with the pink slip
the shame old crap
folks that's all there is

dem' golden years

i spy
bewitched by liz
trekking in starland
the vacuum tube mother

rochester'ing with benny
pairing with paar
riding with bonanza
that's all on four

the black horse paladin
travelling have gun
to johnny yuma
the rebel with no cause

sitting on ponderosa
just hoss'ing around
while hunting for beaver
because father knows best

gunsmoke of lucy
breaking from desi
while honey moon'ing
with jackie and batman

sterling in twilight
zoning with adams
in mansion with fester
worried about munsters

being judged by perry
avenging gomer and hogan
our home grown heroes
showing columbo the crime

ozzie and harriet
having adventures
only dreamed of by jeannie
in her cocoa beach condo

jetson'ing the moon
with my favorite martian
stopping by my three sons
at petticoat junction

my green acres
makes room for daddy
beverly hillbillies riding
in the wild wild west

hiding in dark shadows
with dennis the menace
on gilligans island
with hawaii five'o

brought to the present
by kim and the gang
jane the virgin
not the good wife

orange the new black
hannibal in fargo
louie is younger
the last man on earth

six million dollar man
paid by american idol
real wives of jersey wondering
if americas got talent

ferguson and baltimore
snapped us all back

titles

the BARRIO BOY fucked and screwed
among others OUR NIG who went
DOWN THESE MEAN STREETS passing by the round
BODERLANDS of
THE COLOR PURPLE where he met an
INVISIBLE MAN while the neo-ricans
THEIR EYES WATCHING GOD saw
THE PLUM PLUM PICKERS who said
BLACK NO MORE while the
NATIVE SON preached to the world
I KNOW WHY THE CAGED BIRD SINGS

THE ONLY GOOD INDIANS wanted
to sing while the jukebox was playing
THE WEARY BLUES that is when they decided to leave
the rez and
TELL IT ON THE MOUNTAIN when
the painted INDIAN HORSE took the
ONE WAY TO HEAVEN while driving
his jalopy threatening the rats
WITH A PISTOL IN HIS HAND

THE NEW NEGRO wanted to see
the BLACK SUN rise on tuesday
with ISMAELILLO alone but then

decided to visit the GREEN GRASS, RUNNING
WATER NORTH FROM MEXICO when late last night
FLAVIUS JOSEPHUS told to us about
dam THE NEW JIM CROW that was
printed with THE OTHER BIBLE while
eating BLACK CAKE made sweet
by BLACK BUCK after he took the a
train back HOME TO HARLEM to see
the great BLACK THUNDER standing
on lenox and one twenty-fifth

we were WAITING TO EXHALE
after reading the long
AUTOBIOGRAPHY OF MALCOLM X
when the FIREKEEPER'S DAUGHTER
bought THE PAINTED DRUM while
she shopped at the rez
looking for sales at
THE HEAVEN AND EARTH
GROCERY STORE but finding just
sitting alone the SISTER OUTSIDER who saw but
could not understand
THE ABANDONMENT OF THE JEWS
or THE INDIANS OF BORINQUEN
when they warned us all that day
that CUSTER DIED FOR YOUR SINS

but that never explained HOW THE
GARCIA GIRLS LOST THEIR ACCENT
because they refused to listen and
heard A VOICE FROM THE SOUTH that warned them
about
THE WIND FROM AN ENEMY
while visiting an ISLAND IN HARLEM
to celebrate dance and jazz to
MY BONDAGE AND MY FREEDOM

they told me that my
DRY LIPS OUGHTA MOVE TO
KAPUSKASING and drink the soda
LIKE WATER FOR CHOCOLATE so
they could maybe recover from the last
ONE HUNDRED YEARD OF
SOLITUDE explaining to the peasants
all about the lie and fairy tale
of THE RACE PROBLEM but not
answering or addressing
DID 6 MIILION REALLY DIE
but all the time wondering
WAS MARTIN LUTHER KING A COMMUNIST but
those were some of
THE WATER CARRIER'S SECRET while we all were
growing
UP FROM SLAVERY when we drank
 to much bourbon and ran

the RACE TO THE SUN

RUN BABY RUN if you want to save
your white BELOVED ass when you go
WHERE WHITE MEN FEAR TO
TREAD telling BLACK EAGLE CHILD
all about the broken electrified wired
CIRCUIT that never existed and was
shorted UNDER JUST ONE FLAG

THE SOULS OF BLACK FOLK end this
by denying in the PRISON WRITINGS
of a the lost CIRCLE OF NATIONS
while chanting and crying but not
knowing THE HEARTSONG OF
CHARGING ELK being evicted from
THE HOUSE ON MANGO STREET on that
MONDAY THE RABBI TOOK OFF

ramblings

cups
broken coffee'd
black
memory remnants fragments of
time
aftertasting cancered sweeteners
killing
suicidal movements
hovering
between lies and
untruths

given over
at morning'ed meetings
conjugating
hopeless verbs
buy
sell
con
not being wholly
holy

disbranched souls
dead in living bodies
existing
by yesterday's interest
installments

paid on tomorrows
loans
borrowed by our
grandfathers
on the surety of the
generation
of lost
children

given over to
inoculated perdition of babbling
speakers
computerized by quantized digits
of enhanced orders
given by unpromotable
generals
behind air conditioned
screens
filled with coco puffed
subordinates

transfiguring tomorrow's
casualty list
for capitalized fox'ed outlets of
convulsed flag waving
bageled
latte drinking
couch sitting woke
politicos

9 11

vació
en los calles que camino
vació
en el cielo que miro
vació
en mis ojos que veo
todo que ya no es
vació

en nuestra cama sin ti
solo queda tu voz
en nuestro contestador

a las nueve cinquenta y nueve
minutos
de la mañana

vació
mi corazon que
ahorra
despues de muchos meses
se queda una
y otra vez
una y otra vez
viviendo

a las nueve cinquenta y nueve
minutos
de la mañana

NOTE: Translation by the author
follows.

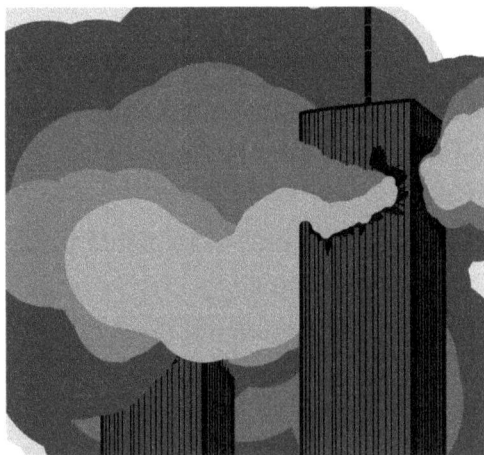

9 11

empty
in the streets that i walk
empty
in the sky that i look
empty
in my eyes that see
empty
all that no longer is
empty

without you in our bed
only your voice remains
on our answering machine

at nine and fifty nine
minutes
in the morning

empty
my heart that
now
after many months
still remains
time and time again
living

at nine fifty nine
minutes
in the morning

CHAPTER FOUR

———

Colored Wars

———

The Fourth Day

greetings

a
fifteen cent'ed
token'ed
tunneled turnstill'ed
trip
down to hamilton

               screw the play

not for play
farting past
forted steeled cannons
balls black

               not my own

mepp'ing naked
down to shorts
then stripping
our commando'd balled broken
dicks
hanging swinging out
with air conditioned
heads
given free

               at high price

our first blood
shots

tear our flesh
then papered pictured dna'd
up
for next of kin
our dear ol' uncle
who for our lives
payed
just one cheap one way
token subway
                    for our futures

oathing in our eighteenth year
kill be dead
who gives a fuck
no questions asked
                    no quarter given

then boarding
bus to train to
turn
this virgin'ed unstained
brooklyn'ed bum
colored boy
to a bloodied tamponed
maggot
                    our forgotten self

basic training

fearing
relief anger boredom
disappointed
mixture of mixed
emotions
gleefully guilefully accepting
happily rejecting
regret

the cold shame of
extensive exhaustion
hot drunk on
homesickness
emptied of numbing
spirituality
filled with salt tableted
prodigious pride
as we
ready on the right
ready on the left
lock and load
one three round magazine
to commence the
ejaculation
of our big black wands

night emplacement

silence

unbroken sand
colored
kevlar'd hardened flesh
descending
under mosquito'd infested
skies
a'lighting lightly on
ancient akkadian meadows

crushed
still born crops
churned
by modern warfare's
prime movers
leaving
browned stringed mutilated
afterbirths
on a diesel fueled muddled
earth

emplacing during sunrise'd
death's darkness
planting trails

holes maybe future
graves

we unshaven shadows of
human self
preparing setting killing
fields
in lands desolate
foreign forgotten

under alien suns
we orphans
blackened
having had historied
lives
yet forgotten fragmented
nows

preparing targets
adjusting
rounds splashing
registering deflections
of all measured
hopes

gps'ed within
five mikes yet
not knowing

who what where why
how

our last lay line

lost

firefight

forty two second
lifetimes
under gunsmoke'd sunlit shattered
childhoods
abandoned silhouetted
as
fully jacketed
peter panning
fairy tailed
nightmares nestle
through the air

above
magic dragon
huffing
leaded death
onto red'ed bleeding
earth

hiding
seeking ditches
ditching in paddies of rice
while airbursts bursting
willy pete and timed
       h   e

pissing past
body armored
kidhood
of fece'd trousered
lives living only
                        the now
like the child
                        lost
puffed
away

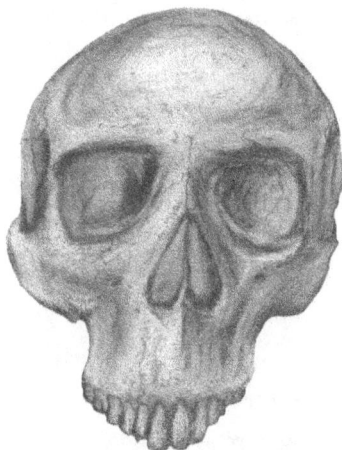

battle buddy

brains yours
                    splattered
on my uniform
                    clean
just returned
ago three days
                    resurrected
from blackened missions now
gray matter yours
                    clumped
                    dangled
                    crucified
strands on my blouse
and body
armor

                    next day
my day
                    off
spent through your gear
                    sterilizing
your crap
before sending
                    home
                    keeping the porn

juicy jackoffs
something you don't need
you

returning   to your wife
nicely package-ed
saran wrap-ed
jfkmlkrfk-ed fuck-ed up
for your flag draped
cargo seat

home
gone
even now   you
screw with my time

services
thoughts to say

brainless
words generals like

to keep us going
over the wire
again

again
we smoke
our after mission 'gars

talking
trash dissing
you
missing you

                at shotgun

missing you

we brief for

                tomorrow

where someone
will get to wear   my
               brains
on their blouse   cleaned
saying the same crap

                same service

for generals who like

                words

who cross the wire

                never

and those who wear uniforms

                never

        never

            get dirty

        never

            get dead

the kill

i
i am lone
i
under starlight
that prisms through my
soul   you
                    you solely
                    you
                    you the other i
                    that lives but dies
i   as i will

i
see you
ranged and windaged
as your head is seared
seared
in my brain   you
                    you for only you
                    i
                    wait unseen unheard
                    undiscovered
                    you
                    you and i distantly dance
                    our dance of death

i   you

                       you pose

                       i

                       take the shot

                       my covered wand ejecting

                       comes completing

                       my desire ending

i   you

i kiss   you

goodbye my humanity

leaves impressed by lands

groves quietly spiraling

with the faint whisper of my finger

    we

    we paint you

                      red

    we

    we see me

                      white

    we

    our souls get

                      blued

        on my

                      kill

painless

trapped crapped
encaged enraged
animal
chained by
uniformed
dressed right dressed
misguided oaths

uncased fluttering colors
secreted
greed bursting over
gently whitewashed
lies

relationships
ill defined
fractured intractable young
hearts
processed trained shipped
morphined numbed
visions
leaving empty casings shells
spent

chalked blackboarded
spreadsheet listed

souls
in camo'd tents
isolated
terror turned
inward
on desert sands
drifting
crackling
three round bursts

unseen other waits
patiently watches
working the windage
then   pulls
getting off
one
full metal jacket
penetrating
fractured sphenoid splintered
occipital fragments
presidentially kennedy'd
into lasting
painless
peace

leave

i
wasn't there
when i came home
with dessert sand
grinding my
unashamed ashened
soul

i left
arms fragmented arms
legs fractured legs
head shots
on my boots
layered
splattered brains
on my blouse

i used
disinfectant cleaner
on my hands
but left my
soul untouched
before we touched

my
brittled bones

brushed down
dirt cleaned
yet
forever imprinted with
memoried nightmares
lost lives
desired

i
only wanted
you your
vagina breasts
the warmth of your
body
maybe too much
not enough

you
wanted more
what i did not have
what i left
in places marked
on my face
on my desert sanded
soul

i
came again

home left again
again
knowing that
i could
never
come home
again

i
left the way i left
you
the first time

you
tell the children
their father
has a new family
one that requires
no feeling
no touch
no hope
no tomorrow

no today

ia drang

the morning haze
bloody
wears away

soldiers
standthose who can
with hollowed eyes
unholy'd

the rest
dead
lie resting from
battle

god's accursed blessed
gift
to his warriors

CHAPTER FIVE

Colored Losses

The Fifth Day

on naming names

once a name i had   i thought
picked peculiarly from
love
they say   somehow
along the way   i think
i lost the
love
i lost the   name

picked up quite a
few along the trip
given by others
in affection   other than

in ol'missip titled i
with the my niggar   name
to honor i
they called

ol'bama gifted i
with the   handle
heyboy you
that them there
charmed

in the lone state star

longhorn bbqed cow
boy
crystal city crackled
appraised was i
wetback   titled
which in brooklynese
transforming the tongue
to fucking
spic
was meant

later in years
private in nam was i   appel'ed
which in oakland
how many
babies
killed   did i
was intent

heard gook
slant eyed
but not at i
but later in the desert sand
other   heard
i

in the taking   names
now

i paint picking
painting the night
dark
under triple canopy
or desert star
lie laying
i call him
charlie or hajji
wanting him dead
painting him red
who i hardly knew

not knowing their first
that some were   named
x they picked as
brother malcom did
y z q t b g l is also
good

he   i
all
painted names

                    nigger spic chink
                    kike coon gook
                    hajji wetback
                    charlie spook

the list goes on

fag queer wop mick
frog redneck whitie

to the ones yet not
chosen
to the new births
not yet named
'til the next vote is
taken
'til the next name is

named

homeless

lying

plastic covered
remnant
blanketed living
corpse
phantom'd soul
trapped in
wars
not wished
remembered not

surviving

cardboarded boxed
beds
bivouacking broadway
vietnam'd
somewhere between
korea and iraq

carrying
shapeless sharpied signs
begging
dignity promised but
not

lined itemed
in next year's budgeted
war

incoming

nickels dime'ing
towards
sidewalked hollowed
eyes missing
aiming at forward deployed
star bucked cups
giving no aid
allowing no
quarters

wounding

two bits
pity begrudgingly
given by
passing citizens
always
absent on
sang crispin's day

displacing

wounds
unpurple hearted
nightmares
unbled sublimating last
hopes

of returning

of finding

home

my lover departs

i
taste

your vaginal
blood
as it splatters
across my mouth
changing your pads

i
see

the color of
feces
staining your panties
while wiping you discharges
with wetted tissue

i
smell

your pungent
body
unshowered
non deodorant'ed
your musking odor

i
feel

rippling rolls of
fat
pressing your belly
injecting chemotic anticoags
into putrefied hopes

i
hear

oral and anal
gaspings
supposits
fending off blossoming
cranial mushrooms

i
cry

with you together
alone
as our
the warp and weft
fractures

we
hold

each other at
sunrise
a friday
morning

your soul flies leaving
me
souless

i
die
i cry
i feel

alone alive

alone

alone

my children

eyes yours
shotblooded
flooding pain
katryning
over levees

fort knoxed fears
guarded quietly
now
rolling thundered
sobbings
on my return

lifetimes
months years
magic dragon
puffed
given to jungle
sand
bullet

unguarded
family reserves
wasted
stolen innocence

battlefield broken
discarded
along with candied wrappers
used
parent teacher meetings
absented
bottle deposits
unrefunded
birthday parties
missed
last years newspapers
unrecycled
babies' first steps
missed
all tomorrow's future
wasted

free at last

mama's teat
daddy's knee
porky pig
donald duck
choo choo trains
g-i joes
gummy bears
easter eggs

love the knicks
those dam mets
new york yanks
pepitone
playing first
richard'son
holdin' two

super'man
green lan'tern
spider'man
basket'ball
high school girls
pick up lines
making out

english lit

motown gals
baby love
calcu'lus
senior prom
ol' man's house
moving out

solm'ly swear
b--c--t
m-six-teen
a--i--t
one-o-one
tiger air
cam ranh bay
vi-et-nam

claymore mines
punji sticks
tunnel rats
fratricide
clean head shot
body counts

tiger force
dexedrine
phetamine
dak'to fight
left alive

back at home
ol' jim bean
good ol'jack
not e'nuf

hero-ined
blind the pain
ma is dead
wife lon' gon'

no v-- a
home'less vet
on the street
all a'lone

pa's shotgun
midnight snack
some ol' crack

all in black
all my soul
all in pain

have no hope
no way out

hemmingway'ed
all my brains

on the wall
trans-fig-ured

free at last
thank god almighty

free at last

NOTE: *The M16 rifle shoots three round bursts on auto*

section sixty

pebbled
limestone markers
stand
labeling lives lost
dressed right dressed
covering fields
of broken promises
all
marked with chiseled alien
battles
giving service to
duty honor country

crew cut grass
greened from ordinance shattered
bodies
enshrined distorted
at pain's unfathomable
depth
all in hidden
horizontal'd
cemented vaulted
boxes
heroes endeavored reward
six feet
below

CHAPTER SIX

Colored Hopes

The Sixth Day

wha's happenin'

i
assuming not knowing
why
why do you ask
not
really wanting to know
not
having common measures
how
should i answer
you

i
could tell lies but
would they work
preserving
the distance we have between
us
or do you prefer the truth
partial
it would be at best
not
wanting to be discomforted

i
will not tell you

in words
nothing
that can be used to help
nothing
you can use to
hurt
so we pass each
other
giving worthless
meaningless expressions of our
pain
meaningless nothings of
our
libeled lives

we
lie pretending to ask
not
wanting to hear
not
wanting to touch each other with
our personal
truth
not wanting

"cool, an' ya"

birthpains

your water breaks
over
your unshaven legs
whore style spread
open
running dripping squirting
cum like wetted
fluid
on your forced open
blackened reddened
vagina

now
your cervix
swells
effaces dilates my name
my touch on your body
a profanity
fucking screaming
cursing
lamazing breathes
hating my
penis

inhaling
locking your arms

stiffly hardened unbreakable around
mine

the cry
blood splattering
comes
over your
thighs
spasming crowing
our wet spot
our violently gentle love
gently
coming to undiscovered
life

cutting the chord
it
ours
cleaned pink

christmas wrapped
swaddled up
turned over to
us

holding hands
holding our connected
future

preferring more
but
waiting for the six week
heal up
before beginning
again a new
creation

beginning's ends

in the center
hallowed space
hollowed
the nothing of emptiness
filled
by edgeless pointless
light

then creating
darkness

expanding beyond boundaries
inflating nullness
condensing matter

you and i
our essential reality
our silence
apart together then
born

apart

what
we are
blind sentients

apparent non-existence
formed in light
warped and wefted
fabricated bounded
together tightly in
blacks and lights

change
late autumn
comes
last leaves falling
beginning
their ending journeys
cycling twisting
changing themselves
through uncertainness
unawares of their
beginnings
unaware of their
endings

unwoven decomposing strands
forming new
life

yet unknown

connections

mosulian evening rain drops
    come softly
    leaving their marks
    never   returning

broadway'd sunny day'd faces
    pasted on
    picture taking boxes
    clicking
    like high heeled whores
    on the street   below

brooklyn blowing turbulence
    birds high
    against the sky
    windy
    seeking newer   heights

on a rainy evening
on a sunny day
on meeting turbulence
diversities from times and places
come together
and you and i become a
we

you and i

      peculiarity in quiet things
      rising sun
      unnoticed important things

become a we

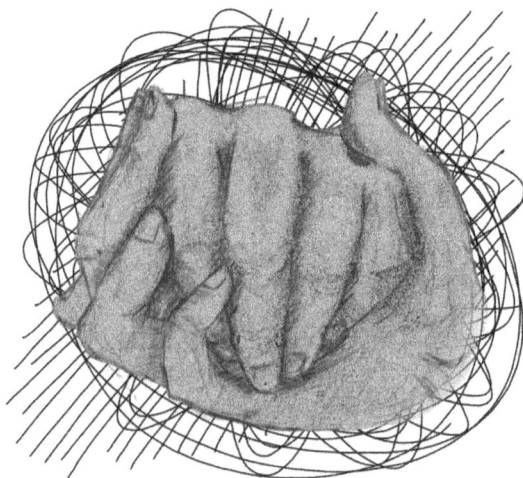

schrodinger's cat

infinitesimally
small detailed
samples
of our passing lives
intertwine
connection our near and distant
not and maybe selves
interacting against each
other
not affecting the
other

purposeful
processing errors
hiding hideous
uncertainty
of life and death
against
unprovable political
equations

the cat
lives
the cat
dies
long live the
cats

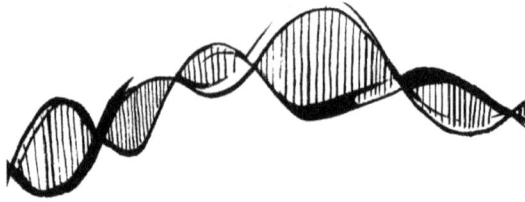

i

am

a man

am

i

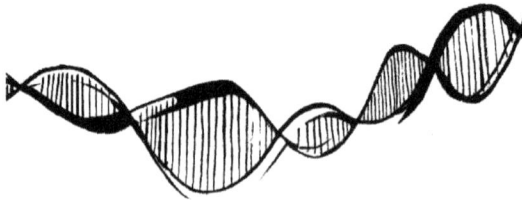

surat al'ikhlas

the descending
winds
cross the desert
rushing
through my soul
carrying the voice of
the prophet
sallallahu alahi wa sallam
through distance space meaning
time

teaching   aleph
as it turns the
earth
preparing it for
seed

it whispers   haa
as it brings the winter
rain
falling gently on thirsty
ground

it instructs secret   dal
blooming flowers breathing
in the dessert

sand
filling the air
with the fragrance of
growth

wind rain earth sand   breath
chanting words of prophets
dervishly wildly whirling
coming together seeding
love
caressing each other bringing'
life

the cradle of forgotten lands
ancient
bringing forth the memories
saying again the ancients
names as   one
enki enlil inanna
again singing the verses of
enheduanna

let it be known
continuing the ancient songs
separating colors of light
past
reforging old paths
anew

praying in the ancient languages
timeless

let it be known
dancing
to traditions of prophets
lighting
the rightly guided
guided the four first

let it be known
accepting
approaching the knowledge
all that has gone before
must go after again
reborn

let it be known
acting justly
loving mercy
walking humbly
with our god
is all that is
required

let it be known
mississippi john hurt
preaching the truth

all
sounding singing prophets

ya' got ta' walk
dat lon'sume valley
wel'
ya' got ta' walk it for ya'self
ain't nobody else
can walk it far ya'
ya' got ta' walk dat valley
for ya'self

to find the one
the meaning

the love

أحد

tikkun

my
eyes closing
letting the hour's annoyance
grievance pain
lap past my
being breath
i

your
one enters my
being
soul spirit
binding
without end with all
that is hidden in
you

i am
that you are me
now belonging to one another
belonging to completeness
united with the you
uniquely the
one

we are

now

hopeful hopelessness

darkness burning

light

flaming my being a'light

etched in black

fire

against the granite stone of my

soul

lettering our name

yours

ineffable unmentionable

the sacred ninety nine

the hidden seventy two

the magic forty two

the four lettered

all

bringing down

the thirty two paths

showing the way

love

אהבה,

CHAPTER SEVEN

One Act
Colored Plays

*The Seventh Day
Sabbath*

an' shit

A one act play

Cast of Characters

<u>VOICE OF CONDUCTOR:</u> Female, off stage. You hear her voice over the train's loudspeaker system.

<u>RIDER 1</u>: White male in his twenties/thirties, dressed in jeans and sneakers.

<u>RIDER 2:</u> White female in her twenties/thirties, dressed in long skirt and boots.

<u>RIDER 3:</u> White female in her twenties/thirties, dressed in a very short skirt.

<u>RIDER 4:</u> African-American female in her twenties/thirties, dressed in business attire.

<u>RIDER 5:</u> African-American male in his twenties/thirties, dressed in blue medical scrubs.

<u>HOMELESS:</u> African-American male in his fifties dressed in old, non-matching rags. He smells very badly as will be noted by the other passengers when he gets on the train.

<u>Scene</u>

New York City Subway, starting at Forty Second Street Station on the Coney Island bound Q line

<u>Time</u>

During the last year of Obama's Presidency (2015). It is about 1100 hours.

This is dedicated to the homeless and nobodies of the world who could be our brothers, sisters, mothers, fathers, husbands wives, or, in another word, just us.

Scene

SETTING: *We are on the Q train heading to Coney Island at about 11:00 am. There are five people in the car, two white females, one African-American female, one white male, and one African-American male. When this is performed in a reading, the character who is speaking will put a small their eyes to indicate that what they are saying is in their thoughts. However, the director may use any other method to convey this.*

VOICE OF CONDUCTOR (Off Stage)

This is the Coney Island bound Q train. The next stop will be Times Square, Forty Second Street. You can transfer to the One, Two, Three, Seven, N, R, or W train.

> *(Rider 1 puts the mask to his face as he speaks as all the RIDERs do. He looks at RIDER 2 and RIDER 3, the white females.)*

RIDER 1

Now those are two fine looking ladies. I would love to bang either of them. Too bad that skirt didn't go a little higher.....I wonder if they're wearing panties..... probably......too bad.

> *(RIDER 5 looks at RIDER 1.)*

RIDER 5

Now that is a fine piece of ass. I wonder if he's gay.....
(RIDER 2 squirms a little in her seat.)

RIDER 2

Shit....my pantyhose are falling.....can't fix it now....
(RIDER 4 looks at RIDER 5.)

RIDER 4

I wonder why that silly ass nigger is wearing scrubs. A doctor? Wouldn't mind hooking up with that. Wonder if he does house calls.
(RIDER 3 looks at RIDER 2.)

RIDER 3

The way she's squirming, I bet her pantyhose is falling. Forty second next? Shit, I hope it doesn't get too crowded.
(RIDER 1 looks at RIDER 2.)

RIDER 1

Look at that girl squirm. Maybe she's trying to masturbate? Naw....I should be so lucky. SHIT....I'm getting a boner....think of....think of....my mother.....SHIT.... that's disgusting...

RIDER 4

Canal Street....Canal Street....I wonder how many stops....my interview is at one...maybe I'll grab lunch down there....hope they hire me....I'd be set if I become an associate at that firm....

VOICE OF CONDUCTOR (Off Stage)

This stop is Forty Second Street. This is the Coney Island bound Q train. The next stop will be Thirty Fourth Street Herald Square. You can transfer to the One, Two, Three, Seven, N, R, or W train. Please watch out for the closing doors.

> *(As the doors close they are stopped by a person trying to get on the train. It is a HOMELESS man. He gets on the train and looks at all the people. Some make a face and others try to discreetly cover their noses as if to hide a smell.)*

HOMELESS

Wat de fuck ya lookin' at............an' shit....
Ya think I's smell like shit............an' shit....
Well fuck ya and the pussy ya came in on.........an' shit...
I's got riet's to sits her and ride dis train..........an' shit....
I's don't giv' a dam wats ya think..........an' shit....

RIDER 4

Oh, lord...save me.....if that smell gets on me......the interview...

RIDER 5

Somebody's gotta introduce that nigger to soap.....

RIDER 3

Dam....I knew it...fucking Forty Second Street.....

RIDER 1

If it wasn't so cold I'd walk.....

HOMELESS

Ya know's it's fucking cold out dere......an' shit....
Ya try sleepin' in a fuckin' shelter.....an' shit....

> *(HOMELESS looks at RIDER 4. HOMELESS*
> *takes a bottle of cheap wine out, unscrews the*
> *cap and starts to sip it throughout the scene)*

RIDER 4

I need this crap before my interview?....oh sweet
Jesus....he's coming this way....

HOMELESS

Fuck ya and yar fuckin' jobs.......an' shit....
I's kuld git wun if I's wanted........an' shit....
Jus' don' wanna work with fuckin' wyte peepul......
an' shit....

RIDER 4

Another ignorant nigger....

HOMELESS

Jus' cause I's black.......an' shit.....

Don't mean I's don't knows shit.......an' shit...

I'm a fucking poet an' do know it.......an' shit....

I's got my shit her.....an' shit....

> *(HOMELESS reaches under his coat and grabs*
> *from his crotch a bundle of papers.)*

But ya's ain't gonna steill my's shit from me ......an'
shit.....

Dey ways ya's dat took my 'istory.......an' shit.......

Ya's gotta pays for dat yet.....an' shit.....

> *(HOMELESS walks towards RIDER 2 and*
> *RIDER 3.)*

RIDER 2

These fucking panty hose.....I should've got a smaller
size....

RIDER 3

Coming this way.....FUCKING FORTY SECOND
STREET.....next time I take a cab...

HOMELESS

Ya' wyte 'oors like ta suck my cock.....an' shit....

Well ya's ain't gettin' any of mise dik'......an' shit....

Ya's need to pay for that kind of shit....an' shit.....

> *(RIDER 1 looks at RIDERS 2.3.4.)*

RIDER 1

Hey....ladies if you want to suck my cock....

RIDER 2

Where is Erma Bombeck when you need her?

HOMELESS

Ya's ain't fuckin' me like jeffirson did did.....an' shit.....
Fuckt' dose nigger gal's leavin' all dose black babies
daddyless.....an' shit.....

> *(HOMELESS walks to RIDER 2 as she stills*
> *squirms trying to adjust pantyhose..)*

RIDER 2

.....maybe if I reach under my belt.....and pull....to many
people and .....dirt man is coming this way.....ignore
him....ignore him....read the advertisements...

HOMELESS

Wy's ya not tryin' to look at me........an' shit.....
I's no fuckin' indivisibl' man......an' shit....
Ya's knows that Ellison wrot' dat shit.......an' shit.....

> *(HOMELESS walks towards RIDER 1.)*

RIDER 1

Shit....he's blocking my view.....cant see her up her
skirt....fuck you, man.....just was getting a boner.....

RIDER 2

Is he getting a hard on looking at me?..

RIDER 3

Is he getting a hard on looking at me?.....

RIDER 4

If that white boy is getting a hard on ....

HOMELESS

Brodar' Langston put'it down......an' shit
And brodar' Malcom' got it ryte.....an' shit.....
By any means nesessari....an' shit....
Dat scart' the wyte ryte off'n yar face.....an' shit.....
But ya capped his ass......an' shit.....
An' ya'll got doc King in the head .....an' shit......
Now ya's scared of a black man.....an' shit.....
Dat niggar in dat wyte house.....an' shit.....
(HOMELESS walks towards RIDER 4)

RIDER 4

That nigger seems to know a thing.....too bad he didn't
trouble himself with an education....could have been
someone....a bad ass lawyer like me working for a
famous New York law firm....GO GIRL, GO!!.....

HOMELESS

See's, I's got an edukashin'.....an' shit....

But ya'll are dumb as shit.......a' shit....

Tryin' passin' Jesus as a wyte boy.....an' shit.....

RIDER 3

What?.....He thinks Jesus isn't white?....I guess he's
never been to church......and blue eyes....

(HOMELESS walks towards RIDER 5.)

HOMELESS

Ya's look like a doctor....an' shit....

An' when ya's give a transfushit.....an' shit....

A fuckin' black man gave ya dat shit....an' shit....

An' washin'tun dc......an' shit.....

A mudder fuckin' nigger plannt' dat' town......an' shit....

(HOMELESS walks towards RIDER 1.)

RIDER 1

What's this shit....an' shit.....hey, that's some funny
shit....he's coming this way
again.....this is fucking affirmative action in action.....he
must think because I'm white I got to smell his shit.....a
fucking nigger loser.....

HOMELESS

I's served in 'nam....an' shit....

Didn't see a lot of wyte folks in the bush over der....an' shit...

I's was mudder fuckin' airborn'.....an' shit....

Bad ass infantry....an' shit....

Kill't plenty of gooks....an' shit....

Did ya' dirty work for ya.....an' shit.....

    (HOMELESS reaches back in his crotch and pulls out a box but just holds it.)

RIDER 1

Vietnam.....airborne....you must be high as a kite....in your mother fucking dreams.....

    (HOMELESS walks towards RIDER 3 but drops the box and nobody notices.)

RIDER 2

That fucking does it....I got to get this fucking panty-hose off. It's is now digging into my fucking vagina.... getting off next stop....

HOMELESS

Ya'll are so fuckt' up...an' shit.....

I's gotta get off dis train.....an' shit.....

'fore ya's fuck with my head ......an' shit.....

An' make me think wyte ain't shit.....an' shit.....

RIDER 2

I'm going to get a dam yeast infection......last time I borrow my mother's pantyhose....

VOICE OF CONDUCTOR (Off Stage)

This stop is Thirty Fourth Street, Herald Square. This is the Coney Island bound Q train. The next stop will be Fourteenth Street, Union Square. You can transfer to the B, D, F, N, R, W trains. Please watch out for the closing doors.

HOMELESS

I's gonna go where people know shit.....an' shit....
But I's ain't tellin' ya where......an' shit.....
'cause ya'll wuld fuck dat up too.....an' shit......

> *(HOMELESS leaves the train with RIDER 2. RIDER 1 notices the box, opens it and reads a paper that is stuck in it.)*

RIDER 1

Private Jessy Smith is awarded the Silver Star for action single handedly leading assaults against five enemy machine gun positions and continuously exposing himself to enemy grenades, machine gun and automatic weapons fire. His actions precipitated the rescue and saving the lives of ten of his men. His actions bring great credit on himself and his Nation.

> *(PAUSE.)*

I be fucked.....an' shit......

(BLACKOUT)

(END OF PLAY)

bullard

all blood runs red

A one act play

Cast of Characters

KKK1: White male twenty to thirties.

KKK2: White male twenty to thirties.

KKK3: Middle aged White male.

WILLY: Middle aged African-American. He is young Bullard's father.

JOSI: Native American female in her early thirties. She is Willy's husband and young Bullard's mother.

YOUNG BULLARD : Eleven year old African-American male.

Scene
Columbus, Georgia USA

Time
Circa 1906.

This is dedicated to all those great known and unkown heroes of our past that made us who we are.

Scene

SETTING: *It is 1906 and we are outside the one room cabin belonging to YOUNG BULLARD'S Family in Columbus, Georgia. It is late at night and everyone is sleeping. The stage is in blackout and we hear and we hear a noise on stage right. Men are talking as they are trying to accomplish something in the dark. We see nothing but can hear their conversation. As the conversation goes on the lights raise slowly but stay dim until indicated.*

KKK1

I can't see nuthin'!

KKK2

Stop complainin' and just stick it in.

KKK1

I can't.

KKK2

You never had a problem before.

KKK1

Well, if I never had a problem before it was because ya' did right what ya' were supposed to do!

KKK2

What the hell you talking about?

KKK1

Your hole is too small.

KKK2

Too small? Maybe your damm thing is too big!

KKK3

What's takin' you idiots so long?

KKK1

Joe's hole's too small to get it all up and straight.

KKK3

Damm it, makes your hole bigger Joe. I don't wanna be out here all night. We got church tomorrow.

>*(We hear a noise that may be a digging sound and a groaning.)*

KKK2

There.....try it now.

KKK1

Yeaaaah! That fits good.....nice and tight.

KKK3

Now put it in the hole and git it all de'way in there!!!!
Ram it!! That's it.

>*(Pause)*

Ready to light it up, Joe? , Joe.

KKK2

Yea...I am all fired up!!.

KKK3

It's party time...LIGHT IT UP!

>*(A flash of light in the darkness on stage*
>*right and we see a burning cross and*
>*three men dressed in KKK sheets. They*
>*all are armed and KKK2 has a whip.*
>*They are passing around a bottle of*
>*whiskey and shouting and hollering.*
>*The light brightens the cabin where the*
>*YOUNG BULLARD family is sleeping.)*

KKK3

Hey, Willy......Why don't ya' come out here and have a
nice and friendly talk with us!

>*(We see the YOUNG BULLARD family*
>*jump out of their beds, WILLY YOUNG*
>*BULLARD, his wife, JOSI, and their*
>*seven children. (Eugene) YOUNG*
>*BULLARD is eleven years old and runs*
>*to the window to look out.)*

KKK1

Yeah, NIGGA....come out and play with us. We got some great toys.

> *(KKK1 cracks his whip in the hair multiple times.)*

KKK3

Willy, if ya' come out quietly we promise not to mess with your kin'. You don't want us to come in a get ya', do ya'?

WILLY

Jacques, get away from that window! Josi, take the children and put them in the root cellar!

JOSI

Willy, what'da they want?

WILLY

They want me. Me and Mister BULLARD had a fallen' out and I guess this is their way to....

KKK3

Willy....Now don't ya're keeping us waiting. Come out and talk to us like a man.

KKK1

More like a nigga...

(The men outside continue to holler and drink wiskey. JOSI runs to WILLY and throws her arms around him to hold him. YOUNG BULLARD goes to a corner and we see he is taking an old rifle and preparing to load it.)

KKK2

We're jus' gonna talk to him, right?
    (KKK1 laughs.)

KKK1

Yeah, we're just gonna talk.

JOSI

Willy, they's gonna kill ya'.
    (WILLY holds JOSI to calm her.)

WILLY

Hush yourself, woman, they ain't gonna be any killin' tonight.
    (PAUSE)
Now, just do what I say and take the childen to the root cellar and wait 'til I come to fetch ya'.

JOSI

I'm afraid, Willy, I'm afraid.

WILLY

Don't be...it'll be awlright...

> *(WILLY kisses JOSI to calm her but as he does he notices YOUNG BULLARD with the rifle going to the window.)*

BOY!! What'da hell are you doin'?

> *(WILLY moves towards YOUNG BULLARD to take the rifle away from him.)*

Ar'ya crazy?

YOUNG BULLARD

Don't worry Pa. I'll fix'em.

WILLY

Boy, you gib'me that damm rifle.

> *(There is a struggle for the rifle. YOUNG BULLARD does not want to let it go.)*

YOUNG BULLARD

No! I'm gonna fix'em up for ya'.....

WILLY

Ya' damm fool!

> *(WILLY slaps YOUNG BULLARD in the face and secures the rifle.)*

JOSI

WILLY!

WILLY

Do ya' wanna get us all killed? Now, woman, do as I says. Get all the children into the root cellar.

> *(JOSI lifts a trap door in the floor and*
> *starts   to shuffle the children into the*
> *root cellar. YOUNG BULLARD is last)*

JOSI

What are you gonna do?

WILLY

I'm gonna go outside and talk ta' dem. See if we can maybe work some'in out.

YOUNG BULLARD

Pa'....

WILLY

Not now, Jacques. Ya' go with ya' mére. There'll be a time when you need to be a man....but that time is not now.

> *(YOUNG BULLARD runs to hug his father*
> *then goes into the root cellar followed by*
> *his mother. WILLY closes the door and*
> *covers the trap door with a rug.)*

KKK3

Nigga, time is up. We's fixing to come in and fetch ya'.
No tell what may happen to yar' kin if we do.

WILLY

I's comin' out misser bullard. No need for ya'll to come
in.

KKK3

Da's a goods boy. Ya' jus' comes out and we can talk.
       (KKK1 cracks the whip a few times in
the   *air.)*

KKK1

Yeah....just talk.
       (The men outside all laugh as they
       continue to drink. WILLY slowly opens
       the door but rushes back in to change
       his shirt and put on one that has badly
       worn.)

WILLY

No need to ruin a good shirt.
       (WILLY walks to the door, opens it and
       stands on the porch.)
I's here miser Bullard.

KKK3

How do you know it's me, nigga. I's ain't Mister
Bullard.

WILLY

I can har' by yar voice, misser Bullard.

KKK3

See there, Nigga. That's the problem with ya'. Ya's a
smart ass Nigga that don't know his place!

KKK2

Can we just get this over with. My wife is waiting up
for me.

KKK1

Let me learn him!
>   *(KKK1 cracks the whip.)*

KKK3

Just wait a minut' befar ya' get all riled up.
>   *(KKK3 walks slowly to WILLY.)*
Ya know I's a fair man, right, Willy?

WILLY

Ya's miser Bullard. Y'as always fair.

KKK3

I told you boy, I's not Mr. BULLARD......but if ya' wanna call me that, ya' can.

WILLY

Yes'um, sur.

KKK1

Can we stop the palaverin' and just learn the nigga some manners, boss?

KKK3

Just, wait a minut'.
(PAUSE)
See, Willy. Yu's put me between a rock and a hard place. These fine church going folk here want to teach ya' a lesson in manners. It has come to the attention of the good folk of the Columbus White People Moral Committee that some of ya' niggas have been getting rather uppity lately.

WILLY

I dint do nothin' misser boss.

KKK3

But ya' did, Willy. 'membered how ya' talked to me......I mean, talk to Mr. Bullard this afternoon?

WILLY

I di'n say nothin' bad, Boss.

KKK3

There ya' go again, contradictin' me again. George...
> *(KKK3 turns to KKK1.)*

Go ahead and lern'im.

KKK1

It's about time, boss.
> *(KKK1 takes the whip and snares*
> *WILLY by the feet with the whip and*
> *drags him off the porch feet first.)*

Ya' gotta learn never to contradict white folk, nigga.
We's always right.
> *(We see the trap door lift and YOUNG*
> *BULLARD come out and crawl toward*
> *the window and look it. As he watches*
> *his father get whipped he starts to*
> *assume a fetal position under the win-*
> *dow and cries.)*

KKK2

Jesus Christ, do we gotta do this?
> *(KKK1 turns and shouts at Willy.)*

KKK1

GET ON YOUR KNEES, NIGGA, AND TAKE IT LIKE A MAN.

> *(WILLY gets on his knees and KKK1 begins to whip him.)*

Do you feel like talking back now, Nigga?

WILLY

No sur misser boss.

> *(KKK1 continues to whip WILLY until his skin breaks and blood appears.)*

KKK1

After how Mr. BULLARD lets you work for him and live with yar' family on his farm you dar' sas him?

WILLY

No sur misser boss.

> *(KKK3 walks over to WILLY and bends over as he kindly talks to him. KKK2 walks to the periphery in disgust.)*

KKK3

Listen, Willy, this hurts me more than it hurts ya'.

> *(WILLY is in great pain, panting heavily.)*

WILLY

Yessum, misser. boss.

KKK3

Don't you see, Willy, we can't be toleratin' uppity Niggas running around in the state of Georgia. Ya' know, boy, my daddy owned yar' daddy and he never had a problem like this in all them years. Ya' might think that just 'cause it's 1906 that things have changed.

WILLY

No sur misser boss.

KKK3

Well, we gotta be sure ya' don't think so.....George.
> (*KKK1 begins to whip WILLY again, with gusto.*)

KKK1

So Nigga, do you think times have changed?
> (*WILLY mummers something in pain.*)

I's don't hear ya', Nigga.
> (*KKK1 continues to whip WILLY as they talk. More skin is torn away and blood drips down WILLY's back.*)

WILLY

No sur misser boss.
> (*KKK3 casually lights a cigar as he talks.*)

KKK3

Did ya' hear, George about that damm new flying machine they invented that flies people in the air?

KKK1

Shit no, boss.

KKK3

Somewhere in the Carolinas. Willy, do flying machines makes ya' think that things have changed?

WILLY

No sur misser boss.

KKK2

For Jesus sake, we made our point all ready.

KKK1

What's de matter, Joe? Ya' ain't got a stomach for this?

KKK2

I don't mind keeping the Nigga in his place but do we have to beat him like this?

KKK1

Ya'r a pussy.

KKK3

No, maybe Joe has a point. After all, we are Christian fearing men and so is Willy. Do ya' think ya' learned your lesson, Willy?

WILLY

Ye'sum, miser boss.

KKK3

It's getten' late and we all got church tomorrow, being the Lord's day and all. Ya' know Willy, we do this because it is the will of G-d. Ya' heard of that earthquake that destroyed that heathen, pagan city San Francisco a few weeks ago.

WILLY

Yes'um, miser boss.

KKK3

Do ya' know why the Lord brought his wrath down from heaven and destroyed that city, Willy?

WILLY

No sur miser boss.

KKK3

Because it was a degenerate city with men sleeping with men....with Niggas goin' around thinkin' they's free.... with naked women sleepin' with men, for money....

KKK1

Don't forget all of the Chinks, Boss.

KKK3

Chinks....Jews...Niggas that don't know their place. Do ya' wanna live in a world like that, Willy?

WILLY

No sur miser boss.

    (KKK3 bends over WILLY, smells him.)

KKK3

Yu's Niggas sure stink. Make sure you wash up before ya' goes to church tomorrow.....Looks like we're done here boys.....

    (KKK3 walks to the burning cross that
    is almost out and stares at it.)

....you take care of this cross Willy....
Give our regards to the Misses and your kin.

WILLY

Yes'um misser boss.

KKK3

So I expect to see you bright and early Monday morning volunteering to pick the crop on the lower 40. By the way, you make sure yar' niggra boy comes to work too. We don't wanna come back and learn him the same lesson we lerned ya'.

(Pause.)

Ya know, ther's been talk about that boy of yar's around town. Maybe we'll come back to talk to him.

KKK1

Gee, Boss, can't we learn his boy now? That was the bes' fun I had since I fucked that mulatto bitch.

> *(KKK1 laughs as he cracks the whip on WILLY's back on last time. WILLY crumbles to the ground.)*

KKK2

Your sick, George. Count' me out next time.

KKK3

'Nuf.....goodnight, Willy.

> *(KKK1, KKK2, KKK3 walk about in the darkness. YOUNG BULLARD bangs on the cellar door.)*

YOUNG BULLARD

Ma', they left and Pa's hurt real bad.

> *(JOSI and the children start to climb out of the cellar as YOUNG BULLARD runs outside to help his father. He holds his father's head in his lap. JOSI stands on the porch.)*

YOUNG BULLARD

Pa....

> *(YOUNG BULLARD cries. JOSI sees*
> *WILLY on the ground and runs to him.*
> *The skin on his back is all torn and*
> *blood is running down.)*

JOSI

Oh, my G-d! Willy! What have those bastards done?

WILLY

I'm OK woman. I told ya' they be no killin' today.
> *(PAUSE.)*

Help me up.

> *(JOSI and YOUNG BULLARD help*
> *WILLY stand as he struggles to get up.*
> *They move to the cabin.)*

JOSI

Ya're back Willy...ya're back is all torn up and bleedin'.

WILLY

It's nothin' but listen. We's gat' ta....

JOSI

We's got to take care of you.

WILLY

No, woman. We's gotta get out of here. We's gotta get
Jacque out of here.

YOUNG BULLARD

Whada ya' mean, Pa?

WILLY

They's be coming after you next, boy. Ya's gotta leave
us for a bit.

JOSI

He can go back to my people on the rez and hide there.

WILLY

NO!...no.. That won't work.....It'll be the first place
they's look for Jacque. His got to get out of Columbus
till this thing settles.

JOSI

I can't lose my boy, Willy.

WILLY

Yu's not gonna loose him, woman. He be back.
But if he don't go, they'll surely beat him and kill him.
.... Is that what ya' want woman?

JOSI

No, but...

> (Josi cries as she runs and holds

YOUNG   BULLARD close.)

YOUNG BULLARD

I's ain't goin' Pa. I's ain't gonna leave .....you or ma.

WILLY

Ya' hush now boy. It be only for a little while. Yu's gotta be a man now and take care of yourself a bit. You can come back in a month or so. It'll be OK then.

> *(WILLY, JOSI, and YOUNG BULLARD walk towards the cabin.)*

It'll be OK then.

> *(JOSI and YOUNG BULLARD cry as they enter the cabin.)*

(BLACKOUT)

(END OF PLAY)

Final Notes

The beginning and end of this work bring us full circle from Langston Hughes to Eugene Bullard. As different as the backgrounds of these two Americans are, they crossed parts in Paris between the World War years. Langston Hughes, due to his literary contributions is more likely to be known by readers but Eugene Bullard should also be known as he has made a unique, "first" contribution to America.

The movie "Red Tails." is about the African-American combat pilots who trained at Tuskegee, Alabama during WW ll. The training was an experiment to see if they had the skill to be fighter combat pilots. In the segregated and racially orientated America of that time, there existed a stereotype that African American men were unable to fight and did not have the intelligence to do things like fly aircraft. The Tuskegee Airmen, along with many other African-American warriors, destroyed that stereotype by their courage and skill in battle.

However, the story of the first African American fighter pilot begins not with the Tuskegee Airmen but in Columbus, Georgia many years before.

Eugene Jacques Bullard was born in Columbus on Oct. 9, 1894. He was born to William O. Bullard, also known as Big Chief Ox, the son of a former slave, and his mother, Josephine Thomas, a Creek Native American. He witnessed his father almost being lynched by the KKK while his brother Hector was murdered by them. His family would spend many nights hiding out from the KKK. During those fearful nights, Eugene's father would comfort his ten children with stories of far away places.

He would tell of places where people were not judged by the color of their skin but by the content of their character. He would tell stories he heard of life under the French where people of color could do and be anything they wanted and did not have to be fearful for their lives. When trouble hit his family, he had to escape Georgia for his own safety. As a teenager Eugene stowed away on a ship heading to England. He wanted to find that place where a man's color did not matter, the places that his father always talked about.

After landing and spending some time in England he moved to France. Shortly after arriving, the First World War broke out. Coming from a place where freedom for a COLORED BOY was extremely limited, he saw in France a place where color did not seem to matter. Tasting it, he understood just how valuable

freedom was and how important it was to fight for it.
As a consequence, this young African American man
joined the French Foreign Legion in 1914 and later the
French Army to fight.

He became an Infantry soldier and was engaged in
many battles, particularly the bloody battle of Verdun.
He was wounded twice in combat but each time he
returned to the battlefield. Eventually his wounds
became so bad that he was medically discharged out of
the French army. For his gallantry he awarded one of
France's highest medals, the Croix de Guerre.

Rather than stay out of the fight, he tried to discover
new ways to join the battle. He took it upon himself to
learn to fly and joined the French Air Force as a member
of the Lafayette Flying Corps. He flew over 20 combat
missions and was confirmed with shooting down two
enemy aircraft. Because of his aggressive combat tactics,
he earned the nickname "The Black Swallow of Death."
The Lafayette Flying Corps had many foreigners as
pilots, particularly Americans. When America finally
entered the war, Bullard, like the other Americans flying
for the French, sought to fly for the Americans.

He was told that as far as the Americans were
concerned "Negroes" were incapable of flying and that
if he wanted to, he could join the American army and
do cleaning and moving work for the American forces.

The Americans, who could not imagine an African American fighter pilot flying for anyone, pressured France to release him from action. Their preconceived bigotry could not bear the proof that their views of African Americans were wrong; that they could accomplish anything like their White American brethren.

Being released from the French Air Force, this true American warrior, wanting to stay in the fight, rejoined the French Infantry. He knew that if he joined the American Infantry he cleaning toilets or officer's laundry until the end of the war. For his heroism, he ended the war with many awards for heroism to include the Knights of the Legion d'honneur.

After the war, Bullard remained in France as a jazz musician and club owner. He became acquainted and played with the great African-American entertainers and writers as Josephine Baker, Louis Armstrong and *Langston Hughes*. Records indicate that Langston worked as a waiter in Bullard's club in Paris. When World War II started, Bullard again found himself in the fight. He joined the French Resistance until he was again badly wounded. The Resistance, rather than take the chance of him being captured, secretly smuggled him out of France to America. During his exit from France into Spain, he met many Jews on the same escape route trying to avoid Nazi capture.

After working many years as an elevator operator in the NBC building, this great American /French Soldier died on Oct. 12, 1961. When he was buried in New York City he received no American honors, there was no bugler playing taps. He was buried without any American military fanfare, but he was not forgotten by all. When the French Embassy in New York was notified of his death, they sent a full military delegation to his funeral to bury him with full French military honors.

Many years later, our Nation recognized his heroism. On Aug. 23, 1994, 77 years from the day he was rejected to fly for the Army Air Corps, he was posthumously commissioned a second lieutenant in the United States Air Force.

Not only was he one of the first combat pilots in the world, he was the first African-American combat pilot our nation produced. He was also the most highly decorated African-American Infantrymen we had. He has earned a seat of honor in French history but also deserves one in ours. His life serves as an example of what we can gain when we, in the words of Langston Hughes, "swim past color" The promise of America is not in the red, the blue or any other color. The promise of America becomes a reality when we eliminate bigotry and discrimination from our hearts, when we see all Americans, regardless of their color, religion, back-ground, political leanings, as Americans.

May the stories and sacrifices of all the heroes in these poems and plays help to usher in the day when the words of Dr. Martin Luther King, Jr. are fulfilled. When all of G-d's children, people of all colors, can hold hands and sing the words of the old negro spir-itual, "Free at last, free at last, thank G-d Almighty we're free at last."

List of Poems/ Plays by Chapter

Chapter Five -*colored losses*
    on naming names
    homeless
    my lover departs
    my children
    free at last
    section sixty

Chapter Six -*colored hopes*
    wha's happenin'
    birthpains
    beginning's end
    connections
    schrodinger's cat
    i
    surat al'iklas
    tikkun

Chapter Seven - *one act colored play*
    One Act Play: ...an' shit
    One Act Play......bullard—all blood runs red

Author's Bio

Normally author's biographies are not long, however, to better understand the poetry and plays of this author, the reader is presented with a more detailed background.

Carlo Orto was born in Brooklyn in the 1950's. His father, "Doc", was of Puerto-Rican and African-American heritage and his mother was second generation immigrant from Poland. Carlo's father, "Doc" despite all the challenges of racism, graduated Medical School in 1929, the only person of Color in his class. Carlo grew up in Downtown Brookly around the corner from the Gowanus projects, a Black and Puerto Rican ghetto. There were many Physicans in the surrounded streets but Carlo's father was the only Physician of Color in the nearby neighborhoods.

"Doc", on his mother's side, was the grandson of slaves, and Carlo grew up hearing his father recount his experiences of racism, as he grew up in the South He would tell stories about how a Colored boy would have to be careful when he walked about in the South. Colored boys were warned to stop when a White person approached and never look them in the eye lest they consider it a challenge to their authority

Carlo was home schooled until age eight and started attending school in the fourth grade. He attended elementary and High School in New York City. His first encounter with the Civil Rights Movement was at seven years old when his older sisters came home from school and asked him if he supported segregation or integration. He had no clue what those words meant.

During his freshman year in High School at the age of twelve he returned home on a Friday in November to the news that President John F. Kennedy was assassinated. During his Junior year, he read and

heard about the assassination of Malcom X across the river in Manhattan.

In 1968, starting college at sixteen, the assassination of Dr. Martin Luther King, Jr. was blasted over the radio. A few months later, Senator Robert F. Kennedy was assassinated. Carlo shook the Senator's hands just a few weeks before at a Brooklyn rally when he was running for President. Also in 1968 the Tet Offensive in Vietnam was blasting all over the TV, newspapers and radio. During his college years, the war was quickly coming into focus as he was seeing his friends coming home in body bags.

It was during these years being Colored came into sharp focus. Incidents like being told that he could not room with his White roommate without permission from his roommates parents or being referred to the school nurse by his dormitory dean because there was something "wrong" with the color of his skin, brought home the fact that there was something different about him. Then there were the personal encounters. A girl he was dating for many months told Carlo after coming back from Christmas break that she could not date him anymore. During the break she showed her parents a picture of him and they forbade her to continue the relationship at the cost of pulling her out of school.

During those years many of his teachers felt no shame in the use of the words like nigger, spic, kike, etc. In writing a paper about the Holocaust in an advanced composition, one of the comments was that his paper was unbalanced. The teacher pointed out the fact that his paper did not include any information about what the Jews did to deserve the Holocaust.

As a haven from the bigotry he found in the many humanity courses, Carlo decide to major in Physics and Mathematics These early experiences could do nothing except make him feel different, not really part of the American dream that he that was supposedly going to be part of.

After college, Carlo joined the U.S Army as a private, was selected for Officer Candidate School and became a Field Artillery Second Lieutenant. He served in Turkey as a Turkish linguist for NATO, and in South Korea as the Executive Officer and Battery Commander of a Nuclear Capable Unit. He was part of operation PAUL BUNYAN in 1976. It was this military experience that helped him established his worth and value as a human being.

After his first tour in the Army he attended NYU-Polytechnic in New York and earned his Ph.D in Pure Mathematics with a minor in Quantum Logic. After teaching for many years he returned to the Army and was stationed at the United States Military Academy during 9-11. In 2003 and 2005 he was deployed twice to Iraq with the 101st Airborne Division (Band of Brothers and Sisters). He was awarded the Bronze Star for Combat and received the Keith L. Ware award for Combat Journalism for the articles he wrote about his and his Soldiers experiences in Iraq. He retired from the military in 2012. In 2015 he earned a second BA degree in Creative Writing from The New School in New York. Since retirement he has taught mathematics at Bloomfield College of Montclair University in New Jersey. He has published over a hundred articles in various fields ranging from military issues, mathematics, religion, ethics, civil rights, astronomy, Judaism, Christianity, Islam, etc. He is the father of 11 children and grandfather to 26 grandchildren.